SEVEN DAILY SINS

Seven Daily Sins

And What to Do about Them

Cecil Murphey

SERVANT BOOKS
Ann Arbor, Michigan

For Cornelia Brackett
Even in death, her influence lingers

Contents

Introduction

"Why, it's adultery, of course," she said.

"Oh, no, murder. Has to be murder. That's the ultimate," Jim replied.

Our discussion had begun with the Bible passage about the greatest commandment. Someone in our study group then asked, "But what's the greatest sin?"

After long debate we finally decided that murder ranked first and adultery second. We had no biblical rules for reaching that conclusion, only individual opinions. We didn't pose any unique questions. Levels and degrees of sin have long troubled Christians. Even the church fathers categorized them. They made arbitrary lists, assigning them various levels and punishments.

By the end of the fourth century, the fathers had catalogued seven deadly sins. Why seven? Why not five or fifteen? Seven has always been the number that signified religious perfection. The ancients spoke of the seventh heaven, seven days of creation, seven days in a week. They recognized seven planets, and they counted seven stages of human development. The sacred number occurs fifty-four times in the Book of Revelation, in connection with the seven churches, stars, seals, and plagues.

The church fathers adopted the number, even

though they didn't always agree on the same list. But by the time of Gregory the Great, they had drawn up a unified list of the seven deadly sins. They first emphasized the carnal sins: lust and gluttony. Then came pride, envy, and anger, concluding with greed and sloth (or laziness).

As theologians studied the realm of moral theology, these seven stood out as being more deadly than others. Pride was recognized as the single greatest sin. That was the first sin. According to tradition Lucifer was cast out of heaven because he raised himself up in pride. What about the fall of Adam and Eve in the garden? The serpent tempted them, promising to make them as wise as God. The couple would know both good and evil. Our spiritual forebears wanted to emphasize not only the deadliness of sin, but to point out that one sin leads to another. For instance, pride gives itself away through vainglory, self-centeredness, the desire for recognition or the constant demand for appreciation. We see it in boasting, in hypocrisy, and presumption. For each of the seven deadly transgressions, the fathers also catalogued the minor evils subsumed under them.

For most of us, talk of deadly sins smacks of old-fashioned threats of hell fire or medieval torture chambers. We recoil from such preaching. After all, Jesus frees us from sin. By his power we've experienced deliverance from those overpowering urges of the flesh that would lead us to sin.

For us, the concept of deadly sins sounds archaic. We no longer struggle with these major temptations of life. We've acknowledged Jesus as Savior, and he has delivered us. We fight out battles over concepts such as discipleship, sanctification, and commitment. Most of us don't need help in coping with the *deadly* sins; we need help in overcoming the *daily* ones.

That's how this book came into existence. The editors, sensing a need to help struggling Christians in their day-to-day living, asked me to write a book on the seven daily sins. I immediately responded positively. Then I asked myself, "But which ones constitute those seven?"

Shortly after the editors contacted me, and while I was still praying about the book, I taught at a Christian writer's workshop. I told the participants about this book and added, "I need your assistance. Will you write down and hand in what you consider the most troublesome little sins in your lives?" Two weeks later, members of one local church also submitted their lists. From nearly ninety responses, I selected seven. Most of them fell rather neatly into five of the daily sins I have selected. These suggestions, along with those drawn from my own experiences, point to the little failures that block many of us from living the abundant life Jesus promised.

For me personally, there's another dimension. Three months before the editors contacted me, I had begun praying each morning, "Lord, make me your person, whatever the cost." I did that after much soul-searching and much dissatisfaction with my spiritual condition.

God began pointing out my own daily sins.

Since then I have continued to face what had seemed to me before to be insignificant short-comings. I'd cut spiritual corners, excuse myself, overlook and ignore what I didn't want to see. Now I'm forced to face divine revelation about my weaknesses.

In offering these seven daily sins, I am offering you part of my struggle to become God's person. I know he answers that prayer only as my inner voice listens to those small failures and works toward correcting them.

Lord, make me your person, whatever the cost.
Amen.

ONE

From Deadly to Daily

DURING THE MONTHS Shirley and I dated, a group of us developed a shorthand way of expressing ourselves—the way good friends often do. We had one special expression, "It's only a little city."

We used that phrase when we talked about the minor sins in our Christian experience—telling white lies, speaking thoughtlessly, or exceeding the speed limit by five miles.

Our teasing came from a story in Genesis, chapter 19. Abraham's nephew, Lot, lived in the wicked city of Sodom, which God had decided to destroy. Divine messengers came to Lot, telling him to flee to the hills without looking back (19:17). But Lot wasn't quite satisfied. He didn't want to run to the hills, so he said, "Behold, yonder city is near enough to flee to, and it is a little one. Let me escape there—is it not a little one?" (19:20). The angels gave him permission but said, "Behold, I grant you this favor also, that I will not overthrow the city of which you have spoken." If you've read the rest of the story, you know that only tragedy and heartbreak follow. Lot bargained and said, "It's only a little city."

When we, thousands of years later, chided each

other with the statement, "It's only a little city," we meant, "It's only a small thing, but look where it leads." And where do these little cities lead? The little white lie becomes the bigger lie that leads to greater acts of deception. The little words spoken thoughtlessly damage our relationships.

Recently I read of a teenager who went on a rampage, killing both his parents and a younger sister. The article quoted interviews with neighbors and even his school principal. Apparently the young man had become the school bully as early as the third grade. In high school the principal suspended him several times because of his abusive language and disorderly behavior. Then came the ultimate result: At age sixteen he murdered three members of his family because he couldn't have the family car. His waywardness started with small things, such as anger and disrespect, and mushroomed into the violent explosion that resulted in the loss of human lives.

In the syndicated column "Dear Abby" a letter from a young women told of dating a fellow named Marty. One time Marty lost his temper and shoved her. He apologized, and she continued seeing him. Later, in a fit of jealousy, he beat her so badly that she ended up in the hospital. She said, "I should have learned my lesson when he first started shoving me around." Abby replied, "If only a few women learn that the most violent beatings always begin with a shove, a punch or a twisted arm, it will be well worth the space in this column" (*The Atlanta Constitution*, Sept. 18, 1980).

When dealing with sins—especially the minor

ones—we seldom look down the road. Someone wisely said, "You do not feel the devil when he first puts his hand on your shoulder." Sin usually starts small and grows. One failure seems so insignificant. But what happens when the second stands next to it? And then the third?

I recall reading a novel of Victorian England in which a woman married and murdered three men before anyone detected her crimes. She fed her husbands a few drops of arsenic each day in their food. Arsenic accumulates in the body, so that the poison slowly spreads until the next dosage proves fatal.

We seldom ever think about the effects of the "little cities" in our lives. The apostle Paul said it this way: "God is not mocked, for whatever a man sows, that he will also reap" (Gal 6:7).

Most of us have moved beyond the big sins. We don't kill or rob or break the laws of the land, offences that would imprison us. We're much more content to spend our time in the "little cities." That's where we trip up. These "little cities" make it difficult to live as Christians who want to follow Jesus Christ. Our relationship with him suffers. In one of his parables Jesus said, "Whoever is faithful in small matters will be faithful in large ones" (Lk 16:10).

Each sin hinders our close communion with the Lord. We're all guilty of them, though they may differ for each of us. Margie's problem is an undisciplined tongue. For Ron it's lack of daily devotions. For Pat it's a habit of foul language. For Karen it's littering the highways with fast-food containers and Coke bottles. For Jim it's smoking on elevators that plainly state it's against the law.

The little sins cripple us in our relationship with Jesus Christ, and they hinder our witness to the world around us. Haven't we all heard people say about a person, "Well, if that's how a Christian acts. . . ."

I know those words. I've heard them (or similar ones) about myself. A year after my conversion, I still possessed a quick temper and exercised it freely. One day I dressed down a man in my office. Another man, Chuck, overheard my words, which included no vulgarities, but were harsh words spoken from a judgmental spirit. For weeks I had tried to witness to Chuck about the Lord. When I finished my tirade, the would-be disciple stared at me. "I never thought I'd hear you speak like that." He left without giving me a chance to explain or an opportunity to apologize. I never had an opportunity to talk to Chuck about God, because he would never listen. I blew it—and over such a tiny "little city."

Or was it so tiny? Perhaps the church fathers knew what they were talking about when they spoke of the deadly sins. They realized how little transgressions can sprout into bigger sins. They recognized that little leaks in our spiritual pipes, if unchecked, lead to flooding later on.

And the little sins creep in so easily. They've often become a significant part of our lives before we've even noticed them. I've already mentioned my temper, which troubled me for years. I didn't recognize it as a temper problem. I got miffed, disturbed, slightly upset, irritated, indignant, but never angry. When confronted, the excuse went, "I'm a frank person." That little statement only covered up a biting tongue that could cut others to shreds.

One evening while trying to sleep, depression overtook me. I prayed, "Lord, take this heaviness from me. Is there anything wrong?" As soon as I asked the question, Dave's face flashed in my mind. He had argued with me about an interpretation of the Book of Revelation. He had picked up his theology from the notes of a famous Bible and spouted off propaganda like an erudite teacher. Finally, I said, "Dave you don't know what you're talking about. You're only parroting somebody else's words!"

Lying in bed, those words came back to me. "But Lord, they were true."

The depression did not lift. "But Lord . . . " and I offered another excuse.

Finally, I said, "Lord, it's such a little thing and Dave's my friend. He'll forgive me. He's probably forgotten it already."

Then I recalled how we used to kid each other about the "little city." Here I was, justifying myself with "It's only a little city, Lord."

After an agonizing hour or more, I finally confessed to the Lord and called Dave on the phone. I put that little sin to death. I came out ahead on that one. I wonder how many others I've overlooked— not that I ought to sit and worry about it. I have enough of a load just trying to hold my own the way it is. But I have learned a few lessons about the little sins that plague all of us.

First, we need to recognize them. Unfortunately, we usually learn the hard way. A loving friend whispers and tells us. An enemy shouts it. Sometimes God troubles our consciences (or our sleep!). Few of us learn about the little sins without experiencing an element of pain. This is especially true for the little sins of our daily lives. We easily excuse ourselves with "Oh, it's so small . . . "

Second, we need to handle them ruthlessly. We can't plea bargain as Lot did: "But it's only a little city, Lord." If we do that, we're bargaining for trouble.

For instance, dust and drought used to plague the South until one bright fellow brought in the kudzu, a plant known for its ability to hold the soil and stop erosion. But the kudzu also kept growing. And it happens to be one of the most difficult weeds to control. Once it gets a foothold, it takes over, killing everything else. Awareness of the potential danger of the little sins enables us to fight and destroy them in their embryonic stages. If we get rid of them early, we won't have to contend with them later.

Third, we need to be on guard. We can't let them start. We must stifle that grumbling spirit, curb our negative attitudes, and stay away from people who make it easy for us to yield to temptation.

Eleanor had to learn that lesson the hard way. Hers was a highly dramatic conversion. She became a truly changed person. Prior to her encounter with Jesus Christ she had been one of those women who complain and grumble incessantly. When she finally gave her life to the Lord, she also found immediate deliverance from that sin.

"I'll never be the same again," she said to anyone who listened. And everyone rejoiced over the marvelous change that had come over the woman. She controlled her tongue. There were no bickerings. She possessed a quiet, tender spirit. But within two years, that old spirit had crept back in. Eleanor began to make catty remarks, small innuendos—so small that hardly anyone noticed. Within another year, Eleanor faced up to the fact that she had once again become critical and complaining. She battled it and still does. Perhaps it will always be a battle. But it has gotten easier for her since she began to watch for signs of it popping its ugly self into her conversation.

Eleanor discovered, as many of us are learning, that we are able to handle the big trespasses. We recognize Satan's bold assaults. We battle and overcome through the Spirit's empowerment. It's the little sins that spoil our total victories.

Fourth, we need to call sin by its real name. As long as we think of it as a failure, goof, mistake, or error, we won't really face up to reality. Sin means missing God's highest will for our lives. It means displeasing God. Unless we use the ugly word *sin* we won't recognize the seriousness of our failure.

In the following seven chapters I share my insights into the "little cities" that we run to. Like Lot, we're often unaware that they may lead us into deadly situations.

At the conclusion of each chapter, please read this prayer:

Lord, make me sensitive to the little sins in my life. Let the Holy Spirit convict me and empower me to deal ruthlessly with them. And, Lord, make me your person, whatever the cost.

Amen.

TWO

Did I Say That?

IN A PREVIOUS congregation we had one member whose sole ministry seemed to be that of producing patience and toleration in us. She had a tongue that repeated every snip of gossip she heard, seldom verifying it, and enjoying the spreading of it.

One deacon said of her, "She'll probably make it into heaven, but the Lord will have to cut out her tongue first." That deacon had a good grasp of practical theology, whether he knew it or not. The lady will probably make it into the kingdom. I think she's got enough of Christ in her life for that. But I'm not sure she'll make it much beyond the front door. Her tongue has become a weapon she uses against herself.

She's an obvious example. In that congregation, it didn't take long before everyone knew about her. They still listened, and sometimes even passed her choice morsels on to others. But the longer she remained a member, the less seriously people took her. Worst of all, she never saw herself as a gossip, although she often became upset when people would tell tales about her.

Many of us know enough about the gospel to realize that if we sincerely love Jesus Christ, our eternal destiny is sealed. We've got our advance reservation for heaven. But what about living in the meantime? What about our day-to-day existence?

I'm convinced that one of the greatest battles we have to struggle with involves our tongue. James 1:26 reads: "If anyone thinks he is religious, and does not bridle his tongue but deceives his heart, this man's religion is vain."

We easily excuse our careless speech. I'm not sure that God intended us to take it so casually. We cast it off as "Oh, that's the way she is." Or "You have to take Harold's story with a grain of salt." Yet I don't think the Bible treats it so lightly.

This casual approach reminds me of Ginny, a college classmate. She filled my ears once for almost an hour. The administration had treated her unfairly. One teacher in particular had discriminated against her because she was female. Two classmates had hurt her by saying unkind things about her. The venom poured out, and most of it centered around Dr. Meade, the president of the school.

That afternoon, Dr. Meade saw Ginny in the library and started talking to her. He explained, I later discovered, the reasons behind some of the things bothering her. The next day I saw Ginny after classes, and she told quite a different story, saying how much she enjoyed college. She thanked the Lord for helping her choose that particular one.

Because I hadn't know about the previous afternoon, I asked, "What about Dr. Meade? You called him a two-faced, irresponsible idiot."

"Did I say that?" she replied.

Yes, she had. In anger, of course, and out of anguish, but she had said it. Worse, however, she didn't remember the venomous words. She shrugged and said, "Oh, I was just a little upset, that's all."

In anger and frustration we all say things we wish we hadn't. But dare we dismiss them so lightly? We even wonder sometimes how we could possibly have said such unkind things.

We misuse our tongues. We all do it frequently. And I've wondered about that. If we're serious in our desire to live a consistent Christian life, we naturally handle the big problems first. But we dare not stop with them. We need to keep moving forward, to pull out the little weeds in the gardens of our lives before they take over and crowd out the fruit.

But many people act as though it's enough to have made it inside the kingdom. To this group heaven symbolizes a fire escape from hell. So they're going to be safe, and that's all they're concerned about. And when it comes to misusing our tongues, why it's such a small thing. "It's only human to blurt out and say things we regret later," one Christian told me.

Yet the apostle James says, "So it is with the tongue; small as it is, it can boast about great things. Just think how large a forest can be set on fire by a tiny flame! And the tongue is like a fire. It is a world of wrong, occupying its place in our bodies and spreading evil through our whole being. . . ." (Jas 3:5-6).

I heard about an incident that happened in Atlanta a few years ago. A bright and attractive divorcee lived in a long row of apartments on Highland Avenue. Every night for two weeks, an elderly man of the congregation saw the pastor's car parked in front of that apartment. The pastor often pulled up as late as ten o'clock, and sometimes nearly midnight. The car did not move until daylight.

The man told a deacon in the church, who told another deacon, who told his wife, who told her best friend, who told the church organist, who told the lead tenor. And the story circulated throughout the entire congregation, raising angry cries and confused accusations.

Two skeptical people did not believe the story. So the next evening they sat in a car across from the apartment complex. Shortly after 10:30, they saw the pastor pull up, park, and go inside. Their furor exploded.

The church, being a congregational type, was ready to call a full meeting of the membership and dismiss that adulterous pastor. They'd make sure that the next pastor was a moral leader.

It almost happened. And it probably would have except that a 76-year-old man died. He had lived alone and had no family. The pastor conducted the funeral. One member of the church remembered something. "Say, didn't he live in that same row of apartments on Highland Avenue? The same section as that brunette?"

He then asked the pastor a few discreet questions. He discovered that the minister had been going to the elderly man's apartment every night, sitting with him until he fell asleep. And then the pastor slept on a cot next to him. No one ever thought of that possibility. One man's tongue almost ruined a fine church. Even more, it almost ruined one caring pastor's reputation and life.

That's an extreme case, of course, but we all misuse our tongue. And, while we don't commit a deadly sin, we hurt other people. We do it in all kinds of ways. We exaggerate, bicker over insignificant things, and complain. Sometimes our silence becomes a lie, when we fail to speak up about something that isn't right. I doubt that I need to write much about the misuse of the tongue. We all know our particular weaknesses. I'd like to suggest some reasons *why* we have such a struggle in this area.

For one reason, our natural tendency is to speak out. In western culture, we admire frank people who say what they mean. Unfortunately, our forthrightness sometimes wounds another. It may help to speak up so that people will know where we stand. But we often do it at the expense of another's feelings. Those of us who have this kind of problem may need to pray the words of Psalm 141:3, "Set a guard over my mouth, O Lord, keep watch over the door of my lips."

Second, if anything goes on in the heart, the tongue quickly discovers it. How many times have we lashed out against a person, without realizing we intended to say something hurtful? This happened to me recently. Two other pastors and I talked about attending a seminar together. When one of them mentioned the featured speaker, I said something like, "That man is a pompous boor."

I hadn't thought that before. Later I wondered why I had said such an ugly thing about a man widely respected in our denomination. Then I remembered—and it didn't take a lot of dredging either. He had offended me once. I don't think he even knew that he had, and I doubt it was intentional—but deep within the recesses of my sinful heart I had remembered the slight. Years later, when the opportunity came up, the tongue said what the heart had felt. Jesus said it this way, "Out of the abundance of the heart, the mouth speaks" (Mt 12:34).

A third reason why we have difficulty controlling our tongues is that we haven't really grasped the second great commandment.

According to Jesus, the first commandment is to love God with our total beings. The second is to love our neighbors in the same way we love ourselves (Mt 22:38-39). Most of us handle the first commandment fairly well—or think we do. Yet, we can't separate the first and the second. If we truly love God with our whole beings, the corollary is that we love other people. "He who says he is in the light, and hates his brother, is in darkness even until now" (l Jn 2:9).

We have trouble loving others because we think that love means having feelings and strong emotion. But love (*agape* in Greek) refers to behavior, not emotions. We behave in a way that expresses care. We practice God's love by our kindness toward other people. We may eventually have affectionate feelings for them, but that is secondary.

I learned this once when a church member showed his dislike for me by behaving rudely toward me in public meetings. Sometimes he argued with me or accused me of impure motives. On occasion he would just walk away rather than talk to me.

I went through some deep anguish over the situation, and wanted to retaliate. I think I would have, except that the Lord showed me what the Bible means by love. I felt no affection for the man. But I could treat him kindly, the way I wanted him to treat me. So I made an effort. I always went out of my way to smile, speak, and act friendly toward him. Once in a board meeting, I actually gave him support.

The man never apologized, but he did change. He finally smiled at me and occasionally took the initiative in greeting me. I know the allegations he made about me in whispering sessions. I also know they aren't true. I decided I would not spend my time putting out the little fires he started with his tongue. The fires died down. I hope they're dead.

It was difficult for me. Some people today may think evil things of me that I'm not guilty of. But those who love me know better. I finally rested my case with the Lord. I knew I couldn't win by playing this man's game.

I haven't totally won the battle of the tongue. Have any of us? For most of us it still remains a critical battlefield, one of the little sins that plague us and force us to keep fighting.

The apostle James says that "whoever success-fully bridles the tongue is perfect" (Jas 3:2). That reminds us that none of us fully guard our lips, totally conquering the looselip syndrome. We need to remember that, because it also reminds us that God forgives us when we fail. The Bible asserts, "Don't misuse the tongue." But when we do, we should confess and ask God's help to resist this temptation in the future.

As I write about the tongue, I remember as a boy watching propaganda films about World War II. One film began by showing a poster of Uncle Sam with his finger to his lips and words below like, "Shhh, the enemy is listening." Then the film had several vignettes about careless conversation. In one segment, a shipyard worker talked freely in a neighborhood bar about the number of ships that were being built and their destination once they were launched. A seemingly innocent neighbor listened carefully and then later wired the information to Germany. The final scene showed the sinking of those ships.

Another portion showed a family, receiving a letter from a soldier going overseas. He didn't mention the exact date of his departure, but added something like "eight days after Aunt Mary's birthday." A listening neighbor figured it out. This man was a Nazi agent.

Maybe we need to keep that poster in mind. "Shhh, the enemy is listening." We need to remind ourselves that words can hurt others. The enemy of our souls uses our foolish words to destroy, disorganize, and to spoil God's work.

As we reflect on the careless use of our tongues, we need to remind ourselves that Jesus Christ can set us free, even from this daily sin.

Lord, make me sensitive to the little sins in my life. Let the Holy Spirit convict me and empower me to deal ruthlessly with them. And, Lord, make me your person, whatever the cost.

Amen.

THREE

Bowing to the American Idol

THE APOSTLE PAUL stood at Mars Hill in Athens, looking at the temples dedicated to various gods. He saw one dedicated to the unknown God. The Bible says, "While Paul was waiting for them at Athens, his spirit was provoked within him as he saw that the city was full of idols" (Acts 17:16).

In our contemporary world, we find it difficult to comprehend the anger and pity the apostle must have felt. We don't believe in idols. We think of idol worshipers as benighted souls, trapped in their primitive understanding and guided by superstition.

Yet we do have a strange god in our culture, an idol that many of us serve, though we don't admit it. We have bowed before his shrine so often, we hardly think of our actions. I suspect that we bow as often as a hundred times daily. We take care of our obligations and construct our world around this god.

How do I know? It's not a brilliant revelation from the Holy Spirit nor a marvellous flash of insight. It comes largely from reflection—and also from facing my former way of life. I'd like to tell you about it.

Shirley and I spent six years as missionaries among tribes in Kenya, East Africa. The Africans, who came from a culture of idol worship, knew of gods who inhabit trees or mountains. I often talked to people who formerly worshiped a spirit they believed possessed certain snakes.

We missionaries brought them light, education, and understanding through the gospel. But we also brought them the American Idol. And we didn't even realize it.

It took me a couple of years to catch on. The Africans, I discovered, watched the missionaries closely, observing how they acted, what they said, the way they related to people. Then they "baptized" the missionaries, giving them new names.

They gave them names which (when translated) meant such things as "a woman who works as hard as a man" or "one who breathes fire when angry." One of the names they gave me was *Omore* which means a happy person. I accepted my new name as quite a compliment. They also gave me a second name, which I didn't understand until later. They called me *Haraka*.

Haraka, a Swahili word, means fast, rapid, quick. A fair description because I do everything quickly, from walking to talking to thinking. That did not sound like much of a revelation. I didn't catch on.

One day, an African leader, Henry Nyakwana said to me, "Ah, you white brother. I love you but you have your idol, too."

"What do you mean?"

"In former days, we worshiped trees, but you wear your idol on your arm."

"My arm?" I asked, not sure what he meant. Then he pointed and I saw it—my wristwatch.

Although he spoke in humor, I realized that I, along with millions of Westerners bow to that idol daily. We call it *time*. This god regulates when we go to bed, when we get up, when we eat, when we attend church. Time doesn't have to be our idol. It can be an ally and a friend. But in the spiritual world, it has become the supreme factor of our lives.

Consider our world. We're caught in a world of instant photos, fast foods, and permanent press clothes. We want a religion that zips along on the fast track. I can think of nothing wrong with conserving time, hurrying to get tasks done. But what do we do with the time we save?

We get involved and committed to frenzied activities. We try to pack thirty hours of activity into twenty-four hours. Then we wonder why we're exhausted and edgy and why tranquilizers sell at a momentous rate today.

In Burt Reynolds' film "Starting Over" one scene depicts the hero having an anxiety attack in a furniture store. His brother rushes to the scene and says to the gathering crowd, "Anybody got a valium?" All the spectators open purses, pockets, and bags and throw dozens of pills at him. The audience roars. Perhaps they roar because they recognize only too well how our fast-paced, no-slow-down world grabs for the miracle of valium to give it relief. And all the while, this idol named time laughs because it has taken us captive.

This is especially true of our devotional life. We haven't time to become saints. We want to grow. We want our religious zeal, but God has to slap it to us as we whizz through the church parking lot. Yet, when I read the writings of the great saints of the church, their devotion and commitment not only impresses me but excites me as well. They not only made time for prayer and study, but they put it at the top of the list.

Martin Luther, for instance, was supposed to have said, "Work, work, from early until late. In fact, I have so much to do that I shall spend the first three hours in prayer." When we read the testimonials of Madame Guyon, Francis Fenelon, St. John of the Cross, and others, we become aware of the paltry level of our own spirituality. They recognized their need to pray. They knew they wanted time with God, despite the pressure of their days. They realized something we fail to take into consideration: God doesn't work like the fast lane of the supermarket check-out lines.

We want our inner selves to grow, but we can't accomplish this goal by depending on dial-a-prayer or by offering God a few random prayers, shot like arrows from a bow. The psalmist says he prayed morning, noon, and evening (Ps 55:17), implying that he knew what it cost to walk close to God. Spirituality has a price tag, and we can't get it at a discount.

Perhaps one reason for the rise of eastern religions—TM, yoga, and other meditative groups—in the past decade has to do with a felt need.

Some seek to divorce themselves from the god on their wrists. They know they want inner peace, contentment.

Most of us can't slice off six hours a day or enter the cloister. Even if we could, we're not sure we want that much religion. Even an hour a day may scare us. Yet, I'm convinced that if we want spiritual fulfillment, we have to destroy the time god that rules our lives. He must be our servant, not our master. We must harness him, rather than allow him to dominate us.

I've had to learn this (and continue to learn it) the hard way. I'm the pastor of a growing congregation, and my writing output probably equals that of many full-time authors. Demands on my time continue to flow in. I could so easily let those pressures disrupt my priorities. I'm certainly not unique. Most of us find ourselves embroiled in more activities than we can handle. And it always seems that the spiritual side of life is the first thing we give up.

A few years ago I determined that my private time with Jesus Christ would not fall by the wayside. I had to have it, not merely to continue growing, but to survive. It's a constant struggle to devote the "firstfruits" of my day to him.

The other day this commitment came to the test. I'm fairly well-organized. I make lists of things I must do each day as well as things I hope to do. But as the demands increased, my time became less flexible. Deciding to forfeit devotional time for a week would have helped everything fit in.

"Lord," I prayed, "I need your help. If I cut my

time with you, I'll never be your person. Help me manage the rest of my daily schedule after setting aside time with you."

I didn't get a couple of things accomplished which I had declared I *must do*. I apologized to the people I let down. They understood. I'm still struggling to juggle my priorities and my time. I've discovered that my inner strength comes from spending time with Jesus. I need him daily. My time alone with him is not optional.

Yet I know people who are afraid to be alone. They can't handle silence. If you wonder whether you're one of them, here's one way to find out. Can you walk into your house or apartment when you're the only one home and not turn on the radio, TV, or record player for half-an-hour? When you're alone in the car, do you have to have the radio blaring away, even if you're not listening?

I have a neighbor who turns on the TV when she goes into the kitchen for breakfast. It does not go off until she turns out the lights at night. Half the time she doesn't watch or listen to it. "It keeps me company," she says. She finally admitted that she doesn't want to be alone. She can't stand silence. I didn't ask her if she ever took time out for prayer and Bible study. I'm afraid the answer would embarrass her. But it saddens me that she fills her life with noise and activity, yet has no time for Jesus.

As a pastor it disturbs me that people know so little about the Bible. They confess their ignorance about prayer. In public worship, if the prayer time exceeds five minutes, we hear squiggling and squirming.

Our world has changed drastically in the past 2,000 years. We see this especially in our level of spirituality. I wonder how the apostle Paul would feel if he came to the United States and stood at the top of one of our skyscrapers. He'd see all the idols erected to the Time God. Almost every bank has one, along with post offices, theaters, restaurants.

The other day I counted the clocks in our house. We have six besides our wristwatches. And only three people live there!

This Time God constantly leers at us, attempting to control us by frustrating us. Yet the psalmist declares, "My times are in thy hand" (Ps 31:15). He knew that God could and did overrule the Time God. That's why we can win our battles with this god, refusing to let him push us from one frenzied activity to another.

Here's a few suggestions about how to fight and win.

1. *Let's schedule our days.* I couldn't get by without a schedule. I plan my activities instead of just letting them happen. As a pastor, I don't even visit people unless they know I'm coming. That saves me time. It means people have a choice of letting me come to their home. We have more control over our lives than we may suspect.

2. *Let's know our speed.* During college I had a friend who always made elaborate plans for what he expected to accomplish each week. By Friday night he felt frustrated. He never completed even the major items, partly because he moved at a slow

pace. He had to complete one project fully before he could even think about another. I'm different. I seem to be able to work at several things at the same time or to move from one function to another. I seldom read only one book at a time. I'm always in the middle of two or three different ones.

3. *Let's learn to say no.* We hear much about that today and maybe need to hear more. I'm learning how to apply the brake pedal in my life. I don't have to do everything or to attend every party, activity, or function to which I'm invited. I made up my mind a few years ago that I'm going to have to miss some things in life.

Tonight the TV guide listed a program I'd like to watch. But after I thought about it, I decided against it. I'm working on this chapter instead. I said "no" to TV so that I could say "yes" to writing. I have nothing against relaxation. I'm not one of those huffing and puffing types who must always be doing something constructive. But in this instance, I had fresh ideas on my mind, and I wanted to finish the chapter. I've missed the program. I'll either see it as a rerun or perhaps not at all. Ten years from now, I won't even remember the name of it!

4. *Let's give up some activities.* Two years ago I resigned from four different committees in our county. All of them are fine organizations, all doing an excellent job. But I felt I could use my time better elsewhere. And one of those commitments I gave up enables me to spend one more night each month with my wife. That leads me to the next suggestion.

5. *Let's plan time to relax.* We need to shut off the pressures around us. We need to waste time, to let go, without worrying about the clock ticking away (that's the Time God again!).

The other night I came home at 5:30 and we ate at 6:00. In that half hour we had four telephone calls—all for me, all hurting people who needed to talk. I made appointments with two of them for the next morning. At 6:00 I took the phone off the hook, and it stayed off until 9:00. I was tired and needed to relax. I wanted to read and to lose myself in a world of my choosing. The next morning I awakened refreshed and ready for a long day that kept me out until close to midnight.

6. *Let's schedule time for Jesus.* I'm a firm believer that Christian growth occurs through what the theologians have called the "means of grace." That is, God has chosen methods for helping us to mature as Christians. These methods include praying, reading the Bible, receiving the sacraments, and attending public worship.

I'm convinced that when we come to the end of our lives, we won't remember half of the things that made us rush so much. Last week I drove to Atlanta, which is normally a twenty-minute drive from my home to the central section of the city. I hit heavy traffic and began to get irritated, feeling time ticking away. Then I laughed at myself, "So what's the rush? If it takes twenty-four minutes or even twenty-eight today, so what? At most I will be three or four minutes late to a meeting that almost never starts promptly." That fact enabled me to relax in the heavy traffic. It took me twenty-six minutes to reach my destination. In retrospect, I wondered why it had unstrung me to begin with.

The subtle pressure to live by the Time God's rules hits us every day. It's one of those little sins that keeps us off balance, the kind of sin that makes us feel we have to accomplish more in smaller amounts of time. We may hear a voice saying that to us. But that isn't Jesus' voice. The Lord says, "Come apart and rest awhile."

As frenzied as our lives may become, we do well to remind ourselves that God is always with us. As one friend used to say of him, "God's never in a hurry, but he's never late either." We can use time—instead of letting time use us. As the Holy Spirit controls our lives more fully, we learn to cooperate with God in making time our ally.

Lord, make me sensitive to the little sins in my life. Let the Holy Spirit convict me and empower me to deal ruthlessly with them. And, Lord, make me your person, whatever the cost.

Amen.

FOUR

The Successful Sin

IF YOU HAD been a Christian during the first three centuries and spoken openly of your faith, what kind of response could you have expected? It's likely that you wouldn't have been able to work because most heathen employers discriminated against followers of The Way. If you did find a job, it probably wouldn't have been much of one. You might even have been called upon to become a martyr. Your own family would have disowned and shunned you.

Despite these trials, the first generations of Christians stood for their convictions. God gave them the strength to carry on. Today, we have quite a different situation. We tend to think, especially in the Western world, that we'll find success in every area of life if we remain true to our faith and if we tell others of our commitment to Jesus Christ. Jesus will give us the sweet smile of success in our business ventures. Because he enjoys blessing his people, he will give us better promotions, higher commissions, and speedier transfers. On top of all that, we'll have bigger homes, larger bank accounts, higher standing in the community. But best of all, we'll get heaven as a reward at the end of the journey. We're ushered into the portals of heaven with the joyous words, "Enter thou into the joy of the Lord, thou good and faithful servant."

By contrast, I received a church newsletter which reported that a Hindu published an article in India which urged that Christianity become the official religion because, as he said, "It's the cheapest religion in the world." The author of the article went on to say, "I know what I'm talking about. Here in India we give all for our religion and often keep ourselves poor in doing so. But I have been to America, and I know that there are millions of professing Christians in that land who spend more for gasoline than they do for God, more for their own personal pleasure than they do for the advancement of the faith they profess."

He didn't say it, but he might have added, "And even though they do very little, their God blesses them and they become richer and richer."

It pays to serve the Lord in terms of the return on material blessings and abundance. We can give frequent testimonials to God's abundant provisions. It really does pay to serve Jesus.

But I wonder. I wonder if that's how God planned it. I wonder if we haven't mixed up our priorities somewhere and misread the gospel story. It especially troubles me when I read that Jesus became poor for our sakes (see 2 Cor 8:9). The Lord himself said that foxes have their lairs and birds have their nests. But he himself didn't have any place to sleep (Lk 9:58). I wonder how we square our affluence with Jesus' statements in

Luke's gospel that the poor are blessed (Lk 6:20ff). I also wonder why this blessing of abundance comes only to Western Christians. Most of us are aware of how our high standards compare with those of other countries where children starve, parents beg, and millions would love to feast out of the garbage from our homes and restaurants. But that doesn't seem to disturb our priorities or make us consider whether we're really so blessed by the god of successful living.

I wonder if we've gotten our Christian priorities mixed up and have headed in the wrong direction. In the Sermon on the Mount, Jesus said not to fret about clothes and food, the everyday things of life. He said that the Gentiles worried about those things. If Jesus saw us pursuing the dream of affluent living today, I wonder what he'd tell us?

Have we understood the essence of the Christian faith as a life of *giving*—not merely giving our money, but giving of ourselves, sacrificing our talents for him?

My friend Betty understands. She received a very enticing job offer, one that she could handle well and that held advancement opportunities. After toying with the idea for some time and praying much, she called the woman who offered her the job. "I'm going to turn you down, but thanks for offering."

The woman asked why.

"I realized that I would have to give up some of my church activities if I did. I'm involved. I love our church and the people, and I think that's more important to me than money."

I applaud that lady! She has not been tripped up by the daily sin of success. "What's a few more dollars," she said, "when it means less time in the Lord's work?"

I discussed my concern over the successful sin with a Christian man who has lived in virtual poverty and doesn't seem to mind. He said, "So many people are living in the Old Testament and not in the New, aren't they?"

Later, on reflection, I admitted he was right.

In the Old Testament, God frequently promised prosperity in the form of heavy crops and rich harvests. He talked of a land flowing with milk and honey. The people expected to have many children, especially sons. They knew they'd have adequate rainfall. But most of all, they'd have long lives.

But we need also to realize why they thought in those categories. So far as I can discover from my Bible study or from reading the scholars, the Jewish people had no revelation of eternal life, at least not before the days of the prophet Daniel. They had no inkling, so far as we can tell, that life went beyond the grave. That being the case, God showered his blessings on them by material advantages.

Don't we read of God pouring out rain on dry ground to show his pleasure (e.g., 2 Chr 7:14)? Elsewhere he promised to keep away the locusts and pests that destroyed crops. The olive trees and vines would produce abundantly. Yet when the nation sinned, there was a drought; their crops failed; animals died; and other nations invaded

Israel. The people knew that God was punishing them.

Many have tried to carry the theology and understanding of the Old Testament into contemporary living. See, they shout, God shows his approval by pouring out wealth, good reputation, and success.

Or does he?

When we read the New Testament, especially the gospels, we find a repugnance of wealth and worldly success. After Zacchaeus, a rich tax collector, underwent a conversion experience, he got busy distributing his wealth. Jesus said that the wealthy have an impossible time getting into the kingdom of heaven. The parable of the rich man and Lazarus makes the point that the rich man got his goodie bag filled full on earth. In the life afterwards, suffering Lazarus gets the feast.

How do we reconcile this? I don't want to suggest that God hates wealth. Or that all wealthy people dishonor God. The story of men such as Cornelius (Acts 10) shows that one could be both a good person and a prosperous one. Here are some things to consider concerning success and prosperity.

First, why do we want success? Why do we want the biggest house, the largest swimming pool, the newest gadget, the most fuel-economic car, the best microwave oven?

That question reminds me of a guy named Bob who graduated from high school with me. He never won any popularity contests. I often felt sorry for him because he usually walked to school alone. Occasionally someone would make friendly overtures, and Bob really liked that. Even as early as third grade, he would reward friendliness with bubble gum, root beer barrels, or cinnamon hearts.

I remember Bob calling me one night. "How about going to the movie with me?" Before I had a chance to answer he said, "I'll buy your ticket and popcorn, too."

I didn't understand it then. But on reflection, I think Bob tried to buy friendship. He bribed people into being kind to him. His material possessions—and he had plenty—became his badge of self-esteem. It's as though Bob shouted to the world, "See what a fine person I am. Look at the money I'll spend on you if you'll be my friend."

Perhaps that's how we sometimes think of God. We like him better and we're more faithful, because of all the good things he does for us.

The second thing to keep in mind is that material blessings can turn us away from God. Remember King Solomon? At first he seems like such an admirable man. He'll make a wonderful king, such wisdom and humility. But as the story unfolds, Solomon changes. He marries wives who turn his mind from God. He gets involved in stables and real estate. By the end of his reign, we hardly recognize him as the favored of God. His possessions have turned him from God.

In Proverbs it says, "Give me neither poverty nor riches; feed me with the food that is needful for me, lest I be full, and deny thee, and say, 'Who is the Lord?' or lest I be poor, and steal, and profane the name of my God" (Prv 30:8-9).

I'll always remember two people who made me

realize the value of those verses. George and Edna had eight children to support on a moderate income. We attended the same church in the Chicago suburbs. Yet they always seemed to have what they needed. When special offerings came around, George and Edna always put their money in first.

One day, Edna said to me, "We used to pray, 'Lord provide for our needs.' Then we began to pray, 'Lord, provide for our needs and enough so that we can help others,' and that's how he's been doing it."

They didn't ask for riches and possessions, but they experienced contentment in their relationship with Jesus Christ.

Third, the most serious problem I see with the success syndrome is this: it speaks of a lack in the spiritual life. When Jesus Christ fills our lives, we don't have the gnawing need for bigger houses and larger barns and heftier bank balances. But if Christ isn't central, something else fills that spiritual void.

The apostle Paul wrote a poignant letter to the Philippians. At the time he didn't know if he would live or die. Yet he said, "For I have learned, in whatever state I am, to be content" (Phil 4:11). This same apostle warned the youthful Timothy that "the love of money is the root of all evil" (1 Tm 6:10). In Colossians 3:5, he plainly declares that the sin of coveteousness is the same as idolatry.

Job, the wealthy patriarch, lost all his children, his possessions, and his health. Yet he cried out, "I have esteemed the words of his mouth more than my necessary food" (Job 23:12). That's what we call Christian contentment. It doesn't demand that we leave aside zeal, ambition, and the move-ahead spirit. But it does demand self-searching. We need to ask, "Why am I working so hard?" "Why do I want more and more?"

Jesus told a parable about a rich man who kept accumulating more wealth. One night God said, "Fool, this night your soul is required of you" (Lk 12:20). The parable gives the obvious impression that collecting all that wealth really did the farmer no good. He died and someone else reaped the benefits of his efforts.

A close friend of mine recently got caught up in the successful sin. It grieved me to see him striving so hard for material success. Twice I tried to talk to him about it. I urged him to seek God about it.

"God wants me to be successful so that I can give more and be more useful," he said. He also explained that he would witness to people with his abundance and declare that God had provided it for him.

One day, I asked him, "When you're daydreaming, just letting your mind flow freely, what do you think about most?"

"About making it. About getting ahead."

"That's what I thought," I said.

"What's wrong with that?"

"I had hoped you'd fill your thoughts with the Lord," I answered.

My friend hasn't quite gotten off the success treadmill, but he's thinking about it. He's struggling with the example of Jesus' poverty and his own striving for wealth. "I'm wondering," he said a few days later, "if I've been moving in the wrong direction."

I don't want to be an I-told-you-so person to my friend, but it's exciting to see him thinking about it. It also makes me search my own heart. What does the accumulation of goods mean to my spiritual life? As I add things, do I feel more tied down and cluttered? As I increase my income, does my contentment with Jesus Christ increase?

Those are the kinds of questions I ask myself regularly. Shirley and I have been praying for a long time about our lifestyle. We already have more things than we need. We have an understanding that we do not buy on impulse. We put off buying an item until we're convinced we really need it. We also constantly check up on our giving. Am I giving joyfully and increasing the amount of offering? We've decided that we never want to be so flooded with bills that we have to cut down on what we give God. Perhaps it sounds as if we've got this all worked out. We haven't—yet. But we're moving in the right direction.

I have a friend who has always been an example to me. His name is Chuck, and I've known him since a few months after my conversion. In many ways, Chuck was my spiritual father.

He's wealthy—probably the most independently wealthy man I know. He's also one of the most generous men I've ever known. I don't know what I would have done without his financial and spiritual help during my college days. Yet in the few conversations we've had about money and possessions over the years, he disclaims any particular need or desire for them. I believe Chuck.

Once he said, "I feel sorry for people who get caught in the trap of needing to make more money. They think that by having more they can be happier. But it doesn't work that way. You have to be happy first, and then it doesn't make any difference whether you have much or little."

Of all the daily sins, Chuck surely doesn't have this one troubling him. I wonder if the rest of us could say the same thing?

Lord, make me sensitive to the little sins in my life. Let the Holy Spirit convict me and empower me to deal ruthlessly with them. And, Lord, make me your person, whatever the cost.

Amen.

FIVE

Leave My Body Out of This

AS A MEMBER of the chaplain's association at a local hospital, I heard a lecture on diabetes and children. The biggest hurdle, the lecturer pointed out, involves making the patients understand a simple concept: that what they eat affects their bodies.

Children have difficulty understanding that the food they eat changes their behavior and the way they feel. As I continued listening to the lecture, I wondered how many adults really understand that principle. If they did, would they treat their bodies differently? I thought of people in our congregation.

One man with severe kidney problems heard this from his doctor: "Never touch Coke or soft drinks again." He's had three surgeries, yet he persists in guzzling three or four carbonated sodas every day.

A woman, diagnosed as having a mild case of diabetes, knew the kind of diet restrictions her doctor laid out for her. But at a recent covered-dish dinner at our church, she ate at least three rich desserts. She must have felt some pangs of guilt because she said to the person next to her, "Well, I probably shouldn't, but they all look so good."

These two people both participate heavily in church activities. They'd be offended if anyone asked if they were Christians. They fail to grasp, as many of us do, that our bodies operate much like machines. They are not only to be used but to be taken care of properly, to be kept in good condition. Yet how many of us are good stewards of our bodies? As God's people, we know Jesus Christ has saved our souls. But we're not always convinced that he wants to save our bodies, too.

We overeat, gorging ourselves with junk food. We move through life without adequate amounts of sleep, and then try to stay awake by using artificial stimulants such as alcohol or caffeine. The most exercise some people get involves walking from their car to a building. Twenty steps later they punch the button for the elevator.

Yet, let a well-intentioned friend say something about the abuse of our bodies, and we scream, "Hey, it's my body!" *True.* They're our bodies. But that's only part of the truth. We are the caretakers. They belong to God. They're his for two reasons: *first*, because he created us; *second*, because he redeemed us—and redemption involves the whole person.

The apostle Paul writes, "Surely you know that you are God's temple and that God's spirit lives in you!" (1 Cor 3:16). A few chapters later he says, "Don't you know that your body is the temple of the Holy Spirit, who lives in you and who was given to you by God? You do not belong to yourselves but to God; he bought you for a price. So use your bodies for God's glory" (l Cor 6:19-20). In that same letter, the apostle also writes, "Well, whatever you do, whether you eat or drink, do it all for God's glory" (1 Cor 10:31).

For at least ten years I read those verses before their meaning began to have an affect on my behavior. One day I awakened to the fact that I put a lot of garbage into my body, and then ran to Jesus, aspirin, or doctors for healing when it didn't function properly. It helped to become aware of the problem, but it took years to change my eating habits.

Slowly Shirley and I eliminated foods from our diet that had no nutritional value. Then we cut out those of questionable value. Gradually we worked on foods loaded with preservatives and heavy doses of sugar. We still do not have a perfect diet, but we're healthier. We have more positive attitudes about life. But most of all, we believe that we please God.

I'm writing this chapter about the daily sin of abusing our bodies not to induce guilt, but to point out one of the neglected areas of our Christian lives. God calls our bodies his dwelling places. In practical living, we have not paid enough attention to this message.

Historically, cultures have treated the body differently. Some have declared, "The body is good, and all instincts divinely given." That school of thought urges us to live, drink, and enjoy ourselves without worrying about the consequences. But we can't live by that philosophy when we acknowledge our sacred obligation to eat and drink *for God's glory* (1 Cor 10:31).

A second view, and one that I hear implied often in Christian thinking, is that the body is evil. I've heard fine Christians speak disparagingly against their bodies. They call the body "this vile flesh" and yearn for the day when they can cast off the restrictive frame. They long for freedom. They either constantly ignore the body or they strive to control it, as though the body operated contrary to the Spirit.

The idea that the body is evil comes not from Christian theology but from Plato and the Greeks. The monastic movement picked this up and spent much energy and time on subduing the body.

Yet in contrast to such an attitude, Psalm 8 reads, "What is man, that you think of him; mere man, that you care for him? Yet you made him inferior only to yourself" (8:4-5). God gave us this body. It now becomes part of the sacred dwelling place of the Holy Spirit.

The apostle Paul in Romans 12:1 exhorts, "So then, my brothers, because of God's great mercy to us I appeal to you: Offer yourselves as a living sacrifice to God, dedicated to his service and pleasing to him." Paul doesn't plead for our spirit's commitment alone but for the dedication of our *bodies* as well. And if we think about the Jewish sacrificial system, we remember that God demanded that animals offered to him be in perfect physical condition. As Christians, who offer our bodies as living sacrifices, do we dare to short-change God?

I remember talking about this concept with a friend two years ago. He sat across the table from me, stuffing himself at one of those all-you-can-eat-for-a-single-price places. He heaped his food on the plate and later went back for seconds. He brought up the subject by saying he had developed arthritis in his knees and could no longer kneel to pray. He felt bad because kneeling held a special kind of reverence for him.

I suggested (and I hope gently) that he had brought it on himself through overeating and lack of exercise. His joints simply couldn't bear the extra weight. "If God didn't want us to eat all this good stuff, why did he make it available to us?" He laughed and took a large bite of fried chicken.

"Dan, if God didn't want us to commit adultery every day, why did he make so many beautiful women?"

He laughed but continued stuffing himself. He finally said, "I was prayed with one night in our sharing group. We asked the Lord to heal my arthritis."

"Did you ever consider that he might expect you to do something to help him along?"

"Like what?" he said, but suspicion was already in his eyes.

"Like eating less, losing weight, and exercising—doing whatever you can through your own understanding and with medical knowledge to prevent arthritis."

"That's the trouble with you skinny guys," he snapped back. "Because you don't have a weight problem, you think it's easy for the rest of us."

He was only partially right. I *am* thin, but I remain thin because I work at it. Controlling my weight holds theological meaning for me.

I may have been a bit harsh on Dan. Yet it saddened me to watch my friend, a person I love, attacking his plate as if he were eating his last meal on earth, doing as one wit said, digging his grave with his teeth. Like the diabetic children, the relationship between ingestion and weight seemed beyond him. Or maybe he didn't want to understand. I'd hate to think the apostle Paul's statement, "Their god is the belly" (Phil 3:19) applies to Dan. My friend simply had not realized that caring for our bodies is part of the practical aspects of our theology.

When I talk to friends about the abuse of the body, it may sound as though I'm making a soapbox proclamation. I hope not. I dislike the kind of teaching that only has negative connotations. Yet I get disturbed when I see my Christian friends mistreating God's temple.

Dan and I ate together on Saturday. The following day he sat in the third row in the early service. Our closing hymn was "Take My Life and Let It Be Consecrated." As Dan sang lustily, I wondered if he really should not have been mouthing, "Take My Life and Let it Be. Period."

And it's not just overeating and eating the wrong food that's a problem. What about smoking?

Medical evidence pretty clearly links smoking with lung cancer. Even if it can't be conclusively proven that smoking causes the affliction, the evidence still speaks strongly. Yet I've talked with confirmed smokers who deny the facts. They laugh and say, "Maybe, but I'm not going to get it." Or they argue about all the other carcinogens in food, from food coloring to artificial sweetner. Then they shrug, "So if you're going to get cancer, you're going to get it." One chain-smoker said, "Well, I've got to die one day and meet the Lord. This is as good a way as another."

Another friend simply said to me, "Just leave my body out of this."

I remember answering, "But can you leave your body out of this? Can you ignore the treatment of your body and still profess faith in Christ?"

"What's one got to do with the other?" he retorted and walked away.

These bodies are God's temples. And we're the cause of their destruction. This applies just as much to constant over-medication (which we Americans do only too well) through diet pills, sleeping tablets, and anti-depressants. Many seem to live by the rule that if one of something makes you feel good, two will be better, and five will put you on top.

I remember once when my little brother and I got a bottle of aspirin out of the medicine chest. I could read the word "aspirin" and I explained to my preschool brother about it. "Mom takes this when she's not feeling well."

Then it occurred to me. "Hey, Mel, I feel all right now. But if I take aspirin, I'll feel better and I'll stay well a long time." And with that, we divided up the almost full bottle and washed the pills down with water as I had seen my mother do. Fortunately, I told my mother what we had done. She made us both vomit. I don't know what might have happened to us if we hadn't.

We treat our bodies with similar reasoning. We forget that they belong to God and that he holds us responsible for their maintenance. In another decade, we'll probably discover all the serious effects of marijuana smoking, but right now all the evidence hasn't been compiled. I oppose marijuana for one basic reason: any time we need an artificial stimulus to pep us up, to make us feel good, to give us a better view of life, we're moving in a dangerous direction. It distresses me that our young have turned to peyote, "angel dust," and glue-sniffing. They haven't found inner peace, so they look for it in an artificial world. And they end up destroying God's special place—the human body.

Yet we Christians continue polluting our cities, rivers, and environment without worry or concern. We breathe and absorb all of this and then cry, "Lord, why do you let people die of respiratory failure? Why do I suffer from all these illnesses?" Treating the body as God's holy temple involves more than caring about what we ingest.

What about the amount of sleep we get? That's one I've struggled with for years. When I first started following Christ, I involved myself in activities six nights a week and loved all of them. It meant that I got only five hours of sleep a night. About that time I heard some evangelist declare, "I'd rather burn out than rust out." Those words fed my zeal, and I increased my activities.

Once someone challenged me, "Don't you think

you ought to slow down a little?"

"Jesus didn't slow down," I said, and then I quoted a portion of an Old Testament verse, "The king's business requires haste" (21:8). Even though pulled out of context, this verse spelled out my philosophy.

But the pace couldn't continue forever. I finally had to do my praying while walking. If I knelt and closed my eyes, I fell asleep almost instantly (and then guilt tackled me). Several times at college, we had protracted periods of prayer during chapel. We knelt and I dozed off every time.

One day as I walked in the early morning through my neighborhood praying, I noticed the gardens. The summer crops had been brought in, and the ground lay fallow. It hit me then that God has designed rest periods for all of his creation. Since then I've tried to get adequate rest.

Another significant factor about the treatment of our bodies involves exercise. As a Christian I was too busy to play tennis or volleyball. At the college I attended during my first year, most of the students took time for recreation in the afternoon. Not Cec—he had too much studying to do. And perhaps I even thought that I was being more spiritual than they because I devoted my free time to studying. Whenever anyone asked me to join in a game, I had a good biblical answer: "Bodily exercise profiteth little" (1 Tm 4:8). It sounded better in the Authorized Version than the Revised Standard: "For while bodily training is of some value, godliness is of value in every way." Hiding behind the King James text made me sound more pious and enabled me to avoid physical exercise.

Not only did I look flabby as I grew older, but I began feeling rotund even though I had always been a skinny kid. Worse, during a five-year period I ended up in the hospital twice with a bleeding ulcer. My doctor was concerned that my blood pressure continued to climb. A few months later I decided I needed to exercise this body. And I did it not only because I wanted to feel better but because those verses from 1 Corinthians had finally sunk in.

After cycling and weight lifting, I tried jogging. I found it suited me, even though I don't think everyone ought to jog. I now run approximately thirty-five miles a week. Often I spend the time in meditation. The greatest benefit of jogging is that it gives me a higher level of energy afterwards. When I'm depressed or feeling low, a six-mile run perks me up, and I come back relaxed.

This happened only recently. During a business meeting a man named Gus said something that I suspected would undermine our evangelistic thrust. I was upset. Throughout the next day I thought about things, prayed for Gus, and phrased responses to him. I wanted to apply the brakes without hurting him. I didn't have much of an appetite at lunch. In the afternoon I went for an eight-mile run. When I came back to the office, the problem with Gus didn't seem important anymore. I didn't say anything, and nothing of an anti-evangelism push developed.

More and more I am reminding myself that I live in God's temple as its caretaker. One day I will have to give an accounting to him of the way I've treated his dwelling place. Not everyone understands my thinking. I wouldn't have understood it five years ago. But I'm growing in this area and becoming more aware that the misuse of my body is one of life's insidious daily sins.

One Sunday I preached about the body as God's holy temple. Afterwards one of the women said to me, "I hardly think that's the proper subject to talk about in church. You make everyone feel guilty."

I don't recall my reply, but I thought of the apostle Paul. In his Second Letter to the Corinthians he said he had understood that he had caused them sorrow in his previous letter. But he added that the sorrow which leads to repentance is godly sorrow. I thought about guilt in much the same way. If guilt causes us to rethink our relationship with Jesus Christ, I don't mind a little guilt.

As I become more aware that Jesus came to save the *total me*, I can't say, "Save my soul, Lord, but leave my body out of this."

Lord, make me sensitive to the little sins in my life. Let the Holy Spirit convict me and empower me to deal ruthlessly with them. And, Lord, make me your person, whatever the cost.
Amen.

SIX

The Sin of Convenience

DURING THE EARLY years of my Christian experience, my wife and I attended a church full of people
who attracted us because of their obvious joy in
worship and in their warm fellowship together.

One Sunday evening, the pastor gave an im-
promptu invitation to "come to the altar for prayer
if you have a spiritual need." Although this was a
new experience for me, I responded. For several
days I had been wrestling with a decision about
my career. After two years of teaching in public
schools, I sensed that God wanted me to move
toward the ordained ministry. It both excited and
frightened me. I had talked to no one about it
except Shirley, and I needed guidance.

Perhaps twenty people came forward and knelt.
The pastor walked behind us. He laid hands on
each of our heads, prayed aloud a simple prayer
that God would answer our cry and fill our hearts
with peace. After he prayed, each person got up
and walked back to the pew.

I felt no peace and no comfort. I remained for
two reasons. First, I hoped that God would give
me peace. Second, I assumed that the pastor
would come back and at least talk for a moment

about my concern. Suddenly, without being able to stop the flow, I began crying.

The pastor asked the congregation to rise. He pronounced a benediction and the people filed out. I stayed in front, so burdened with my own need that I couldn't leave. Minutes later, the pastor called out, "I'm going to turn off the lights now," and disappeared. He never asked me then or later about my problem.

I don't think he was an evil man. Either he had no sensitivity or, as I decided when I got to know him better, he simply did not choose to be inconvenienced. He had been invited to a birthday celebration that evening and wanted to get there quickly. In the meantime, I knelt in front, heavy-hearted, struggling with an overwhelming burden, and I needed him.

We're not always so obviously insensitive to other's needs as that pastor was to mine. With most of us, we often don't see other people's problems because we don't choose to see them. It's easier not to notice, or if we notice, not to pursue the matter. We even excuse ourselves by saying, "I didn't want to intrude" or "Helen could have told me if she wanted me to know." Yet sometimes the person hurts too much to take the initiative. Perhaps they don't know how to unburden their soul to another.

More recently, a church group invited me to speak at a midweek program. The committee member who telephoned me had raved about their love and friendliness. When I arrived, I understood what she meant. People obviously enjoyed each other. All over the large fellowship hall, little clusters gathered, sipping tomato juice. The noise level alone indicated the degree of their interaction. Occasionally a person left one group and joined another.

I stood inside the door, waiting for someone to notice me. No one did. After a few minutes I felt embarrassed and sat down on a folding chair. I checked my watch. A full five minutes lapsed and still no one came near. I got up, walked to the serving counter and took a plastic glass of tomato juice. Finally someone talked to me. A woman brushed against me as she laid her empty glass on the counter and said, "Oh, I'm sorry." She moved quickly back to her group.

At last the woman who had invited me must have seen me, although I noticed her when I first arrived. "Oh, you must be Cec Murphey," she said and smiled. She introduced me to two people and walked away and joined another group. Those two people mumbled a few sentences and then walked away. I stayed by myself until the meeting began.

Standing there, clutching my plastic glass, trying to look as though I wasn't bored or lonely, I thought about Jesus' words to his disciples, "If you love those who love you, what reward have you? Do not even the tax collectors do the same? And if you salute only your brethren, what more are you doing than others? Do not even the Gentiles do the same?" (Mt 5:46-47).

Even in the churches where the love of Jesus Christ finds its highest expression, Christians sometimes shower their love only on their friends. After a person has become a member of the group, they love him or her, too. But what about outsiders? What about those who never make it into the inner circle?

In most fellowship groups and church meetings I attend, most people rush to their close friends as soon as the leader pronounces the benediction. The strangers make their way quickly out of the building alone. And why shouldn't they? No one notices them. No one gives them a friendly smile or engages them in conversation.

I'm convinced that one of the daily sins of the church today isn't that we don't love. It's that we're too selective about the people we choose to love. We respond to people like ourselves. We reach out to those who live our lifestyle and are more within our economic circles—the folks we've known for ten years. It's safe in our inner circles. We're comfortable. So we stay right there. It requires effort to move outside our community of relationships, so we close our eyes to strangers.

I remember an American couple who came to visit us when we were missionaries in Kenya. We stopped in a small commercial center for gas, and they saw dirty children, almost naked, fighting over the division of a single banana. The wife turned her face. "Oh, I hate to see things like that." So she didn't look.

That's how many of us react. We turn our eyes away from whatever is unpleasant. We're not quite as cruel as Marie Antoinette. As the story goes, probably untrue, when told that the people had no bread to eat, she said, "Let them eat cake."

Our sin shows itself as indifference, the ignoring of needs. I've often wondered if that's not very much what the apostle had in mind when he penned 1 John. He says, "He who says he is in the light and hates his brother is in the darkness still" (2:9) or "But he who hates his brother is in the darkness and walks in the darkness, and does not know where he is going, because the darkness has blinded his eyes" (2:11). John often makes strong statements, sometimes saying them in their most potent form, and this is one of them. In his usage, *hate* doesn't mean what we take it to imply today. For John, anything less than love was hate. That included indifference, lack of concern, unresponsiveness to a need.

Most of us love and want to love more, *but on our own terms*. We're all for telling Jesus and the whole world, "We want to love people." We also want to add, "but, no inconvenience, please." We want to open the door of caring by our choices. We want to choose those that we allow to invade our private spaces. We want to give a helping hand to people we like. But when we set conditions, it's not really love at all. It's what the apostle terms hatred. It's hatred because it's less than love.

I can think of a vivid illustration of this point. The story as told to me took place on the campus of a graduate school of divinity in the Midwest. At chapel one morning, a professor preached about the good Samaritan who found the half-dead Jew, applied what medications he had, and took the man to the nearest hotel. The preacher ended with an exhortation to care for the hurt and needy.

The next morning, ten minutes before chapel, someone approached four theological students separately. "The professor is sick today and wants you to rush over to chapel and fill in. You can use any sermon you want." Each of the four rushed toward chapel. On the way, each passed a cyclist lying on the ground with blood on his face. All four hurried on to chapel to preach.

Is that a true story? I don't know and the man who told me couldn't verify it, but it has the ring of probability about it. We have our priorities, our tasks, our choices, and we don't choose to be inconvenienced or upset as we fulfill our duties.

Yet, when Jesus talked about the end of the world and the final judgment, he told a parable. He said he would separate the sheep from the goats. He applauded those who visited the sick, who fed the hungry, and clothed the naked. But he gave no accolades to those who only loved their friends.

It's easy to understand why we put limits on our love. Some people spark our generosity. It's not hard to love them and to respond to their need. I'm learning that I have to make an effort to like others. Whenever certain individuals call on the phone, my immediate reaction is, "Why me, Lord?" When I catch myself thinking that way, I ask God's forgiveness. They're God's children, too. They need loving. And maybe they're the ones we need to reach the most.

During my early days as a pastor, our church had nine elderly shut-ins. I tried to visit each of them every two weeks. My secretary called the day before to make sure they would be there and that they felt up to having me. Eight of them made my visits uplifting and a pleasure. They seemed genuinely glad to have me and we established endearing relationships.

But Madeleine was the ninth. I really hated to visit her! A couple of times I skipped her and how she complained! Yet when I sat in her living room, she grumbled about everything. Finally, I determined to get beyond merely doing my duty to Madeleine as her pastor. I prayed often for her. Even though she never changed as long as I was in the church, I did. I began to see her as a woman who did not understand how to love and perhaps needed my visits more than the other eight.

I still struggle with "inconvenient loving." But I've learned a few lesssons, which I'll share with you.

First, I can't respond to every need—even if I want to. Some are more obvious and demand immediate attention. I'm learning to pray more about the needs around me, especially when a situation involves people that don't fit into my inner circle. I think of Paul's words about Jesus: "though he was rich, yet for your sakes he became poor so that by his poverty you might become rich" (2 Cor 8:9). I'm asking God to help me as an individual and to help our church as a local body to become aware of needs that we can meet.

Recently our congregation became involved in caring for the mentally retarded. None of the families in our church have retarded children. Our service started because two people had a burden. One of them works with the retarded. The other was a psychiatric assistant at one time in his life. They saw the need. They prayed, and we, as a congregation, opened our hearts. We call this ministry The Love Class. The class excites me. Of all the people we'd naturally shun, it's the retarded, yet we have a staff of six volunteers (and a few others on call) who have said, "We want to help."

Second, as servants of Jesus Christ, we don't have a choice. It's his decision for us. If we faithfully follow the analogy of servant/master, we don't even have the right to argue with him.

Years ago I picked up a chorus somewhere, which goes, "For who am I that I should choose my way? The Lord shall choose for me. 'Tis better far, I know, so let him bid me go—or stay." That's how we overcome the sin of hatred—we give Jesus Christ the right to make the decision for us. Then we obey.

Third, love means inconvenience. It means surrendering privacy and private space. It means driving six blocks—or six miles—out of our way. Love does what is needed because it's needed.

Once my wife and I planned to attend a retreat together. The day before, a member of our congregation died. I decided to stay to conduct the funeral. But I didn't want my wife to miss any of the conference. I knew a Christian on the other side of town who also planned to attend the same retreat. I called her and asked, "Could you give Shirley a lift?"

"I already have another passenger," she replied.

Later I talked to another Christian who said, "Well, we're already four in a small car. If Shirley doesn't mind squeezing in, we can find room for her somehow."

As Jesus might have asked after that, "Which of those do you think loved his neighbor?"

Finally, obedience brings Christ's approval. Before I was a pastor, Shirley and I used to drive a family with half a dozen pre-teens to church. We had to go three miles out of our way to get them. Some Sunday mornings, we'd arrive and honk the horn. After a lengthy wait, a window would open and a head would stick out. "We overslept today, so go on. We can't get ready in time."

For almost a year we went through that—Sunday morning and again Sunday evening. And it was a burden. But we did it. Every time we prayed about stopping, we felt God wanted us to keep on. The family never offered money toward gas. They never seemed to think of our inconvenience (and we had to get our two babies ready besides). Then we moved away and lost track of the family. Years later we visited our hometown and spent the weekend with friends. Our hostess took care of a small baby. I was in the kitchen when the mother came to get the child.

The mother beamed when she saw me and said, "I'll bet you don't remember me." Of course, I didn't, not even after she told me her name.

"You used to pick us up and take us to church every week. That's when all four of us came to know the Lord. We're all serving Christ now and active in our various churches."

That time I got feedback (even though nine years later!), and how I thanked God that we kept on going back, week after week. I know now that it was worth it. I didn't know then. And I know Jesus approved of our being inconvenienced.

As I think about that incident, I'm wondering if that's the kind of thing Jesus meant in his parable in Matthew, chapter 25. I like to think that I can hear the voice of Jesus whisper, "Come, O blessed of my Father, inherit the kingdom prepared for you" (Mt 25:34).

It's not always easy to love. But then, the Lord didn't say it was. But he did say, "By this love all men will know that you are my disciples" (Jn 13:35).

Lord, make me sensitive to the little sins in my life. Let the Holy Spirit convict me and empower me to deal ruthlessly with them. And, Lord, make me your person, whatever the cost.

Amen.

SEVEN

Are You Here, Lord?

SIX OF US flew from Atlanta to Costa Rica for a week to assist missionary friends. We landed in San Jose as scheduled. But our friends were not at the gate to meet us.

I checked to see if it was possible to telephone them. But they lived 200 miles into the interior and were without a telephone. After discussing our dilemma with the others, I sent a telegram, which would reach my friends by the next morning.

The airport cleared out, and there we were—six wearied and frustrated Americans, knowing less than ten sentences of Spanish and unsure of what to do next. We huddled together as a group for prayer. We prayed individually, but all six of us felt pangs of anxiety and unease.

Late that evening, our friends the Bennetts came to meet us. They arrived in time for what they thought was our scheduled arrival—and it was, originally. But we had sent a letter in plenty of time to tell them of our change of plans. We wrote just before Christmas and arrived in early January. Later we learned that the postal service virtually closes down during the Christmas holiday season.

During our five-hour stay at the airport, I felt a

sense of panic and unease as we waited and wondered what to do. Yet if you had asked me, "Hey, Cec, do you believe that you're going to heaven?" I would have answered "Yes." I would have asserted my faith in Jesus Christ and in all his promises and in my ultimate destiny. It was just that right then in those few hours I suffered pangs of anxiety. I trusted God for the eternal issues, I just wasn't so sure about that particular moment.

I called it nervousness. After all, I had the care of five other people on my mind. I had something to be worried about. As I think about it now, I wonder if Jesus wasn't smiling and saying, "Oh, you of little faith." I trusted him with the eternal questions; I simply couldn't trust him for the present, awkward moment. That's how many of us live—in a state of anxiety. We know God is out there. We're just not sure he's available for the present emergency.

With the perspective of hindsight, I easily chide myself on my nervousness. Our friends came. God didn't let the airlines strand us. The trip turned out well.

In fact that incident has actually become a faith-building experience for me. God came through. He didn't let us down. Each time I go through an experience of that sort, it strengthens me to weather the next storm.

The accumulation of such experiences actually illustrates a sound principle of education, one I used myself on many occasions.

Years ago while teaching in the public schools, a number of teachers tried an experiment that involved dividing the students with high I.Q. scores from those with low scores. I took the students in the latter group.

Most of them had difficulty reading, so I spent most of each day for the first three months teaching them to read pre-primer books and then first grade material. Eventually, most of them at least read on their own grade level.

They also had difficulty with arithmetic. They did computations fairly well, but the story-problems baffled them. Each day we would play a game in the class. I would print six story-problems, divide the children by ability into small groups, and let them compete with each other. It took two weeks before one of the children said, "You know, this is fun."

They had to learn that once they could read the problems, they could do them. It took repetition, getting used to reading a problem, and then reasoning out the answer. When they took achievement tests at the end of the year, they did quite well in arithmetic reasoning. And why not? We had gone over story-problems day after day. They no longer feared such tests.

I think God works a bit like that with us. Each time we suffer from anxiety and worry, we muddle through it, only to see in retrospect that God was there all along. The next time we'll be less afraid and more trusting.

That's one lesson I've learned about handling anxiety: Every time I'm tested, I learn something from the experience. I may not pass each test with flying colors, but I do learn to trust, and my fear dissipates in the process.

A second thing I've learned about dealing with immediate anxieties is that God often speaks to calm our anxieties. But because we're not always attuned, we don't always recognize his voice.

In the early 1970's I traveled to Mexico with five teenaged boys from our church. On the way back, the defective steering of our rented station wagon finally caused an accident. Fortunately, there were no injuries, but the car couldn't be driven. We were several hundred miles from home.

That feeling of where-are-you-now-that-I-need-you-God started crowding in. But before I could say anything, one of the teens—the most unlikely of all—put his arm on my shoulder and said, "Don't feel bad, Preach. At least we know the Lord's with us, don't we?"

Those simple words hit me. Of course God hadn't left us. There were no injuries. Nothing really serious had happened. The car was insured. Within two hours, we had a different car and were on our way back to Georgia. That one sentence was what I needed to hear. It made me aware of God's presence.

We often sing about God's love and protection. But unless he reassures us of his presence in some way, we fret or worry.

I used to think that this kind of anxiety was a problem only for the new believer. Now I suspect it afflicts those in the growing stages as well. The more we participate in the Christian life, the more we expect, and perhaps demand that God will be obviously present to us at every moment.

One of the daily sins of modern Christians centers right there: We can't live with the daily frustrations. We pray daily and read our Bibles faithfully. We give offerings sacrificially. Then why isn't God doing his thing? We're certainly doing ours. I suspect that many of us have become like spoiled children. We expect things to go our way. When they don't, we think that God has to account to us.

As we mature, we realize that nothing ever works out perfectly. Plans go awry. Relationships deteriorate. People change. And often we don't understand why. We need to learn that God doesn't owe us an explanation. Hundreds of things happen to me that I don't understand and may never comprehend. I've learned not to respond to them simply by saying, "Well, I'll understand it all up the line somewhere." What if I don't? Does my relationship with him depend on whether he explains everything? Or do I trust even when I can't get answers or explain situations?

Trusting in God enables me to live in the interim between conversion and culmination in heaven. I've also learned that I can apply Romans 8:28 *and* 29 in my life: "We know that in everything God works for good with those who love him, who are called according to his purpose. For those whom he foreknew he also predestined to be conformed to the image of his Son."

God doesn't promise to work out everything nicely for us. But he does work with a plan in mind that includes us: so that we might be "conformed to the image of his Son." He wants us to be like Jesus.

Whenever I occasionally experience real anxiety, that passage offers me comfort. God's purpose is at work, and I'm going to end up stronger and spiritually healthier because of what I'm going through. That enables me to rest. I can't regulate airline schedules, prevent the blowout of an almost new tire, stop traffic jams on the expressways, or make sure that other people will be as punctual for appointments as I am.

As God's people we do what we can to change our circumstances. But we should realize that we sometimes reach the end of our resources.

Members of Alcoholics Anonymous pray what they called the serenity prayer:

God, grant me the serenity to accept the things I cannot change, courage to change the things I can, and wisdom to know the difference.

As we cope with anxiety, we can also remind ourselves that God uses frustrating circumstances to help us mature.

Once I attended a writer's conference at which they seated me at the head table. I knew all of the others present and would have enjoyed being with any of them except for one man. I didn't like his style of writing or the kinds of things he wrote about. Nor did I particularly like the man himself. And where did I end up but at the end of the speaker's dais, sitting next to the one person I didn't like. He was the only one close enough to talk to.

I began feeling depressed, thinking I ought to

find an excuse to leave the speaker's table. I felt sorry for myself. Then I had the good sense to pause. "Okay, Lord, I don't like this arrangement. But it's settled and I can't change it. Help me make the most of it and see it as a chance to grow."

It took twenty minutes for me to learn to appreciate my neighbor. He turned out to be pleasant, a little shy, and an excellent listener. Best of all, he has since become a close friend. We often laugh about the seating arrangement. He confessed that he had as much reluctance about sitting next to me! For both of us, God used the experience as one more step in our Christian growth.

Another thing occurs to me regarding the sin of anxiety. Most of us want to walk by sight rather than by faith (cf., 2 Cor 5:7), because sight is easier. But the apostle tries to explain that part of our commitment to follow God means that we will obey him without seeing what's ahead or without fully understanding his plan.

I tried to illustrate this principle to our congregation recently. In our worship services, I always give a sermon for the children. This time I asked two boys to assist me. I blindfolded them, turned them around a couple of times, and said, "Okay, boys, now walk back to where you were sitting."

One boy bumped into a wall. The other stumbled around in the wrong direction. After a few minutes, I took their hands and led them. Then we talked about the experience. One boy said, "I kept worrying that I'd fall down."

The other said, "I got scared of looking silly to

everyone, but when you took my hand, I didn't worry."

God wants us to be free from anxiety. And our freedom does not come in one giant step. It unfolds gradually. Perhaps that's why Jesus talks about anxiety a total of six times in one passage from the Sermon on the Mount:

> "I tell you, do not be *anxious* about your life, what you shall eat or what you shall drink, nor about your body, what you shall put on . . . And which of you by being *anxious* can add one cubit to his span of life? And why are you *anxious* about clothing? Consider the lilies of the field. . . . Therefore do not be *anxious*, saying, 'What shall we eat?' or 'What shall we drink?' or 'What shall we wear?' . . . Do not be *anxious* about tomorrow for tomorrow will be *anxious* for itself. Let the day's own troubles be sufficient for the day" (Mt 6:25, 27-28, 31, 34).

God's around. We may not always feel a chill on our spine, a lump in our throat, or goose bumps on our arms. But God stands close by.

I remember many years ago I went through a difficult time in my spiritual journey. God seemed so distant. I kept praying for the Lord to show himself to me. That morning, in my devotions, I read Hebrews 13:5, "I will never fail nor forsake you." God spoke to me in that verse. No bells went off. I felt no emotional charge. For at least a week, I continued in a state of emotional numbness. But Hebrews 13 made the difference. He had promised his presence. I had only to accept it. The Bible didn't say I had to *feel* it. Hebrews 11:6 says, "And without faith it is impossible to please him."

Lord, make me sensitive to the little sins in my life. Let the Holy Spirit convict me and empower me to deal ruthlessly with them. And, Lord, make me your person, whatever the cost.

Amen.

EIGHT

Let Me Prove It, God

ELSIE SITS IN the nursing home in her wheelchair, and I go to see her once in awhile. Because of a number of problems she cannot live at home with her only daughter. Elsie has accepted that reality and adjusted fairly well to the nursing home. Yet each time I visit, I leave depressed.

No matter how the conversation goes, somewhere during our time together, Elsie always says, "If only I could work for the Lord here, I wouldn't feel so bad." Once in awhile she talks to her nurses about God or gives them a scripture passage. She frequently tells other patients about Jesus Christ. When they will listen, she is overjoyed.

But most of the time Elsie feels depressed because she's unproductive. "I used to work so hard for the Lord, you know," she said on my last visit. "I played the organ for more than forty years, and I taught Sunday School a long time, too."

I've never been able to comfort Elsie about this because she has never grasped a fundamental aspect of Christian theology. She bases her value largely on her spiritual output.

By contrast, The Westminster Confession of Faith takes a totally different kind of approach.

This historic document, written in 1647, has become the creedal statement for Presbyterian and Reformed churches. The shorter catechism of the Confession asks as its first question: What is the chief end of man? The answer: Man's chief end is to glorify God, and to enjoy him forever.

For most of us, the answer doesn't say enough. We're willing to say those words, but we want to add to them. We want to add the word "by" and then tack on the proofs of our love. We aren't satisfied to say that our chief purpose is to enjoy and glorify God. We want to say that we glorify and enjoy God by our activities, by reaching many people for Christ, by praying faithfully, by reading the Bible daily, by giving our money to others.

None of us can really add "by" to the statement and have it be meaningful. That's Elsie's problem. She can't accept the fact that she's loved, that she's pleasing to God just as she is. She feels a need to be productive for God if she is to have any value as a person and as a Christian.

As soon as we add "by" to the statement in the catechism, we automatically find that we don't measure up. God's acceptance of us is God's grace. And when we add anything to grace, it isn't grace anymore. Perhaps an illustration will help.

The other day I visited Jim in the hospital. He had undergone major surgery after a severe car accident. But in the whole process of accident and recovery, Jim has surrendered his life to Christ. We prayed together and in one of the first prayers of his life he said something like, "And God, I'm going to follow you now. So please love me."

Afterwards I tried to explain that he had already found acceptance. "God already loves you, Jim, and you don't have to ask for that."

"But I've done so many wrong things."

"That's why Jesus died for you," I said.

In his head at least, Jim knows the truth. But his heart may not be quite as clear about it. He still wants to prove his worth to God. A couple of days later he said, "When I get out of this hospital, I'm going to show God that I mean business. I'm really a changed person."

I suspect that God is as patient with all of us as he is with Jim. Of course he didn't need to prove anything. And I'm hoping he'll understand that one day.

In our society, so many of us struggle for self-worth, for acceptance, for someone to tell us that we're okay. God's been saying it for thousands of years in the pages of the Bible. We just haven't been listening. His message still says, "Come to me . . . I will give you rest" (Mt 11:28). "Leave all your worries with him, because he cares for you" (1 Pt 5:7). The list of verses becomes endless because God says the message in hundreds of ways. But the good news is so good, we can't believe it.

The biggest pitfall in our desire to add "by" to the statement in the catechism concerns the implications of this attitude for our day-to-day lives.

1. *We're always on stage.* That means we're constantly trying to convince God how much we love him. We do our best to make him love us more.

One minister I know learned this lesson a few years ago, after he started to worship in our church, though he had been ordained by another denomination. George had only recently gone through a divorce. He felt shunned by his ministerial colleagues. One of his parishioners said, "If you can't rule your own house, how can you rule the house of God?" George resigned and moved to our city, where he lived with his parents for a year.

During that period, while in the process of re-evaluating his life, George came to a startling conclusion. "God loves me," he said. His eyes glowed and he said, "I don't have to do anything for him. I used to think that if I worked hard and made him proud of me, he would love me more. Now I've discovered that I'm loved just because I'm me."

Until that time, George thought that God's love for him depended on how much he pleased God. His problems didn't vanish from that point, but he finally understood grace.

2. *We put our emphasis on a zeal for theology.* I wonder if the apostle Paul (prior to his conversion) didn't find himself caught there. As a true Pharisee, he zealously guarded the laws and practices of his fathers and meted out death and punishment to violators.

Spiritual pharisees still live in our world. I went to seminary with a man named Rod, who fancied himself Mr. Valiant-for-Truth in *Pilgrim's Progress*, only more valiant. He knew the doctrines of our faith, and he had them all sorted out in his head. He had few problems distinguishing proper actions from improper. When a question arose, Rod always gave a definitive answer, usually based on a passage from the Bible. He carefully corrected anyone who digressed from orthodox theology. One classmate quipped, "Rod sees himself as the guardian of the faith."

For a few years after seminary, I followed his career through friends who lived in the city where he became pastor. Rod preached learned sermons. He taught the great truths of the faith. But did he really love people or understand God's grace? Only God knows. But if he didn't, he could end up like the man in Matthew 7:21-23 who came to Jesus at the last judgment. He expected acceptance and praise, but as he listed his record of achievements to the Lord, Jesus responded, "I never knew you."

We're not known by God because we can list our honors and medals. As we acknowledge his lordship and live in service to others, we *express* our love for him. But we don't need to *prove* it.

One of my favorite portions of the Bible is found in Deuteronomy, chapter 7. That's the story of God selecting the nation of Israel as his special people. He tells why he chose them:

> For you are a people holy to the Lord your God; the Lord your God has chosen you to be a people for his own possession, out of all the peoples that are on the face of the earth. It was not because you were more in number than any other people that the Lord set his love upon you and chose you, for you were the fewest of all peoples; but it is because the Lord loves you (Dt 7:6-8a).

That doesn't really explain things, yet it is the total explanation. That answer says, "We are valued for who we are, not what we'll become or because of our potential." We are loved and chosen by the God who loves us simply because he loves us. Our faithfulness in producing good results neither increases his love, nor diminishes it if we fail.

How does this work out in our daily living? If we acknowledge God's love for us purely on the basis that he chooses to love us, we can rest and exclaim, "Thank you, Lord." We don't need to prove anything. We don't have to increase our output for Jesus, our service to the church. We don't have to head a committee in order to alleviate our guilt or to gain acceptance.

Such knowledge provides true freedom in Jesus Christ.

What about the housewife with small children, who says, "By the time I take care of two pre-schoolers all day, clean house, and cook meals, I'm exhausted. I don't have the energy left to do much in my church while my children are small." God loves her just as she is and demands nothing beyond her ability to fulfill.

Another person works twelve hours a day and goes to school part-time. He says, "I want to do more for the Lord, but . . . " Is God such a hard taskmaster that he demands more?

Many cite reasons why they're not more involved in the local church. One woman works with retarded citizens. Another person devotes ten hours a week to the cancer society. Still another works as a "pink lady" at the hospital. And Jesus loves them all.

I'm not offering excuses for doing nothing or for slackness in our service. But we all find times in our lives when we're not productive. It has no effect on God's acceptance of us.

In the early 1970's I found myself in a situation where my official ministry required less than thirty hours a week. (I had been working nearly seventy.) I went through a bout with depression. Questions about my ability, my worth, my usefulness to the Lord came up. Failure nagged me, and doubt nipped at me.

This continued for seven months. Finally I resolved the situation by realizing that my need for a life of heavy activity had more to do with my style than with my relationship to Jesus Christ. That's when the passage from Deuteronomy, chapter 7, meant the most to me. I felt as though God said, "Cec, I didn't select you because of your ability or your leadership. I love you because I love you."

Can you think of any reason why God should love you? If you can, you haven't understood grace at all. Grace means that we have no claims and can perceive no reason why God would choose us. We merely accept his love.

Jesus told a parable (Lk 18:9-14) which begins with these words: "He also told this parable to some who trusted in themselves that they were righteous and despised others" (18:9). In the story, the Pharisee, the religious leader of the day, stood by himself and thanked God for his own goodness, his service, dedication, and faithfulness. In effect he said, "God, you're lucky to have me."

The publican, a tax collector despised by respectable people, prayed, "God, be merciful to me, a sinner!" Jesus ended the story with these words: "I tell you, this man (the publican) went down to his house justified rather than the other" (18:14).

That's the principle of grace again. The publican saw no value in himself and therefore received from the Lord. But the Pharisee, proud of his productivity, said, "See, I'm really quite a fine person." He missed God's grace completely.

We don't need to prove anything to God. We only need to accept what he offers.

I wish Elsie would understand this. It might not make her days any more productive as she sits in that wheelchair. But if only she could realize that God loves her as much today in the wheelchair as he did forty years ago when she taught Sunday School and played the organ.

What is our chief purpose in life? To love God and to enjoy him forever. Period. Amen.

Lord, make me sensitive to the little sins in my life. Let the Holy Spirit convict me and empower me to deal ruthlessly with them. And, Lord, make me your person, whatever the cost.
                                                        Amen.

A Concluding Word

"I'm depressed," he said matter-of-factly.

We all stared at Barry, not sure what to say. All of us were young Christians, and Barry had been our spiritual leader. His smile and energy had always inspired us. He was ready with the answers whenever we posed questions. Most of all, he cared about each of us. Somehow depression and Barry didn't fit together.

"I've been a Christian now for five years," he said. He stopped and stared at his hands, almost as if he didn't want to see our eyes. "Five years," he repeated, "and look at me."

"I'm looking," I answered, trying to inject humor, "and you've got the same handsome face you had yesterday."

"I don't mean outwardly," he answered and flashed a smile only to add, "but inwardly, I'm a washout. A spiritual zero."

Barry told us how awful he felt about himself, without listing specifics.

"Exactly what are you saying?" I finally asked.

"I'm a Christian and probably know the Bible as well as anybody. I study it every day. I never go to sleep without having had prayer time. But I'm still a spiritual failure." It took Barry twenty minutes to explain to our group. We were all Christians, excited about our faith. For the last several months we had been meeting regularly. And we expected the Christian life to move from one glorious step upward to the next.

While we all cared about Barry, none of us connected his situation to our own. After all, we hadn't felt depressed since we had become Christians. I remember that incident from the early days of my conversion, and now I can understand better.

Barry went through the kind of experience that many of us encounter in our Christian lives. We reach a level of spiritual understanding in which we know the facts of the faith. Jesus Christ no longer talks to us as infants. We teach and provide leadership to others. We become (consciously or not) examples to younger believers.

We want to obey the will of God. But we don't. At least we don't always. If we sit and think about it too long we may become depressed. We keep telling ourselves, "By this time I ought to be living on a higher spiritual plane." We read books implying the ease of victorious living. Preachers frequently exhort us to be perfect. And we don't measure up! That's when depression strikes.

We forget one basic fact of the spiritual realm: *we're still sinners*. God's spirit lives in our hearts. We've experienced his leading. He whispers of his love and forgiveness. Yet we still have to deal with the inborn nature in all of us. The apostle Paul, in a revealing passage, cried out, "I do not understand my own actions. For I do not do what I want, but I do the very thing I hate" (Rom 7:15).

It's a phase we all experience as we move forward with Jesus Christ. In the beginning of our spiritual pilgrimage we move with confidence, almost abandonment. We rejoice in the power of the Spirit at work. Then we hit our spiritual wall.

Recognizing that spiritual wall prompts me to write about the seven daily sins. Your seven sins may not be the same as those I've described. But I hope I've listed enough of the common ones so that somewhere in this book you've said, "That's me, all right."

The message is not one of self-condemnation. None of us lives a perfect life, because only one perfect person ever walked this earth. The point is simply that we don't live up to all the spiritual light we know.

The message of this book reminds us that God has sent his Holy Spirit to us. He knows our weaknesses, our proneness to sin. We can call on the Spirit in the midst of the little sins. And we can be delivered from them. We won't be perfect. But we keep trying because we have a spirit within us that says, "Be perfect . . . even as your heavenly Father is perfect" (Mt 5:48).

Recently Skip spoke at a meeting, and I found his words helpful. Our Sunday school class sat around a campfire after a weiner roast. Skip shared with us his own struggles as a Christian. "I've learned that it's a two-way street," he said. "I used to think that walking with the Lord meant that I had to run up the hill in order to meet God who was already up there waiting for me. Recently I've decided that while I'm running up, God is coming to meet me."

That's the real key to understanding the Christian experience: we don't struggle alone. Through the presence of the Holy Spirit, God is reaching toward us. He says to us, "Don't give up. I'll help you."